Teach You to Swim

With sketches by the author

By Kathryn Paulk

Copyright © 2020 Kathryn Paulk

Table of Contents

Introduction 3
My Background 5
Teach Your Child to Swim 7
  [1] Moving in the Water 8
    Get Into the Water 11
    Walk In The Water 18
    Float on Your Back 25
    Feet on the Ground 26
    Doggy Paddle 27
    Jump In 28
  [2] Swimming in the Water 36
  [3] Swimming Fast 39
    Swim Teams 43
    Advanced Swim Lessons 52
    Additional Support 53
Acknowledgements 57

INTRODUCTION

This book is a set of guidelines for parents to help them teach their children to swim. The guidelines are based on the approach I used to teach my son to swim. By the time he was three-years-old, he could jump off a low diving board and swim to the side of the pool, all by himself. He enjoyed swimming so much that, with dedication and hard work, he became an excellent swimmer.

You don't need to be a good swimmer to teach your child to swim. The most important thing you can do is, simply, get into the water with your child and have fun. Keep your child safe and comfortable. I'm a good swimmer, but I only taught my son to doggy paddle. He refined his swim strokes by taking swimming classes, private swim lessons, and simply swimming a lot.

Only if a child is comfortable in the water can he or she take the next step and learn to swim fast. With support, my son became a very good swimmer. Some of his high school swimming records remain unbroken. At college, he swam on a Division 1 swim team. He currently lives in an apartment complex that includes a lap pool, where he continues to swim on a regular basis. When I visit him and we go for a swim, his beautiful swimming still turns heads. I proudly tell anyone who will listen, "I taught him to swim!"

Many people have asked me how I helped my son to become such a good swimmer. This book is my answer. The things I did are outlined in this book.

My Background

Before I taught my son to swim, I taught many children and adults to swim. I was a lifeguard and swim instructor during my high school and college years. I was a Red Cross Water Safety Instructor (WSI) which means I was qualified to teach swim lessons and life-guarding lessons.

At college, I worked for the physical education department where I was a lifeguard and teaching assistant for swimming classes. During classes, I demonstrated the various swim strokes.

Eventually, I found my niche – teaching the true beginner swimmers. Most students took the beginning swimming class to learn how to swim. However, some of the students were afraid to get into the water. I was usually asked to teach the true beginners – those who were afraid of the water. I developed my own techniques to help these swimmers to overcome their fear of the water and to be safe in the water. My goal was to get these students to jump off the diving board. swim (doggy paddle) to the side of the pool, and climb up the ladder. If they could do that, they would be safe in the water.

The techniques I learned to earn my WSI certification, did not help with teaching fearful adults to swim. With trial and error, I developed my own techniques. Many years later, I used many of those techniques to help my son become comfortable and safe in the water.

TEACH YOUR CHILD TO SWIM

Teaching a child to swim can be divided into three parts:
- [1] Moving in the water.
- [2] Swimming in the water.
- [3] Swimming fast.

Part 1, moving in the water, is the focus of this book. It includes activities a parent may do to help a child become comfortable and safe in the water. Any child who feels comfortable in the water will enjoy it and that is the foundation of a good swimmer. This is an important first step for any child.

Part 2, swimming in the water, is briefly discussed. Standard swim lessons are offered at most swimming pools and provide an excellent way for a child to learn proper swimming techniques.

Part 3, swimming fast, describes the progression of a child from a good swimmer to a great swimmer. Parents of young children, who demonstrate some skill in and a passion for swimming, will appreciate the suggestions included in Part 3.

[1] Moving in the Water

Getting into the water and moving around is the first step in learning how to swim. The goal is to get the swimmer to be safe and feel comfortable in the water.

If you want your young child to enjoy swimming, they must feel safe and secure. Swimming should always be a good experience.

I do not like those methods, where babies are thrown into the water. Instead, I think it is better to hold your child at the edge of the water and let them simply kick the water. Let them set their own pace. Let the child decide when he/she is ready for more.

When my son was just 3-years-old, I had planned to take him to watch a Disney on Ice show. Before watching the ice skaters, I wanted him to know a little about ice skating. Since I had a bad knee, I was not able to ice skate with him myself. Instead, I asked a private ice skating instructor to just hold his hand and, basically, just pull him on the ice so he'd know a little about ice skating. Instead, the instructor placed him in the middle of the rink and asked him to move towards her. He waddled a little, but eventually made forward progress and got to her. Then she gradually moved backwards, causing him to move more on the ice. In a few minutes, he was ice skating! I was amazed.

If I had taught him to ice skate myself, it would have been like lessons from most parents – just hold his hand and drag him around the ice. Since his introduction to ice skating went so well, I signed him up for more ice skating lessons (bucket brigade) and he eventually joined a hockey team.

Age 3
Ice Skating

My approach to swimming is similar to the approach used by the wonderful ice skating instructor. Let the child get the feel of the water and figure out how to make progress. Don't push or pull. Make sure the child is safe and comfortable. Proper technique may be taught later. Throughout this section, I describe the activities I did with my son to help him feel safe and secure in the water.

Age 6 Hockey Stop

Get Into the Water

If possible, start early with young children. Fill your bathtub with a few inches of water and let your child play with a wash cloth and some plastic toys.

Before your child can walk, hold them in your arms by the side of a pool and let them kick the water with their bare feet. It's a simple thing to do, but it is a lot of fun! Children enjoy kicking the water while sitting on their parent's lap.

After children can walk, they usually enjoy walking through water sprinklers. Any outdoor activity with water is fun. Set up a short water slide, if your child is more adventurous. Squirt guns and water balloons are fun too. Playing in an inflatable back yard pool is always fun.

Many public pools have toys for young children to play with. If your pool does not have toys, bring your own plastic toys. Also bring some buckets and unused paint brushes and paint rollers.

Children enjoy painting water on the deck of the kiddie pool. If your child prefers to play beside the pool, that's fine. If the parent goes into the kiddie pool, the child is likely to join them

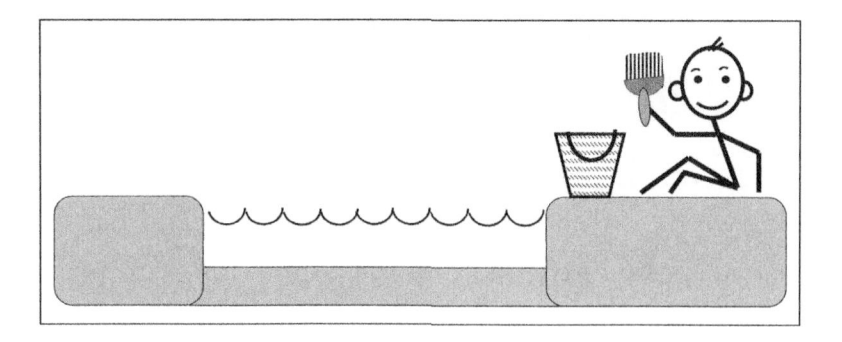

When the child shows an interest in going into the kiddie pool, parents should play with their children in the pool. Of course, allow plenty of time for your child to play with other children too. Start playing with toys that float. Your child may enjoy sitting on your back while you gently move around the kiddie pool, like a friendly alligator!

At this point, children will avoid putting their face in the water. That's fine. Don't force them to put their face in the water. In fact, your objective should be to keep their face dry and out of the water. They should feel safe and know that you're on their side and will help them to keep their face out of the water. They should feel they can trust you. Feeling safe and comfortable in the water is much more important than putting your face in the water. Many parents, with good intentions, often encourage their child to put their face in the water. I think this is counter-productive because it is stressful for the child.

After your child is more comfortable in the kiddie pool, start playing with toys that sink. Your child should still be able to reach the toys without putting their head under water. Never force your child to put his/her face in the water. Instead, ask your child if he/she can blow bubbles under water (with eyes and nose still above the water).

Demonstrate how to blow bubbles, though your mouth, with just your mouth in the water (eyes and nose above the water).

Even if your child can put his/her face in the water, I recommend a high quality **face mask**. Having water in your eyes and nose is uncomfortable. It is much more enjoyable for the child to wear a well-fitting face mask. Go to a scuba shop and buy the best face mask that fits your child. Make sure it does not leak so your child is comfortable.

This was the turning-point for my son. After I bought a good face mask for him, I could not keep his face out of the water. It was such an exciting and comfortable experience for him. He became fearless with his face mask. It covered his eyes and nose. He just took a big breath and stayed under water as long as he could. Eventually, he found the large face mask to be cumbersome so he switched to smaller swim goggles.

Using a pool ladder to get into the water is a scary thing for both adults and children who are fearful of the water. Beginner swimmers may try to walk down the pool ladder as they walk down steps. Climbing down the pool ladder is something they may have never done before so show them how to do it.

Walk In The Water

When your child is comfortable in the one-foot-deep kiddie pool, take them with you to the shallow section of the big pool which is usually about 3 feet deep. Pools usually have adult swims, when only the adults are permitted in the pool, with and without a child. The adult swims are great because the water is less chaotic. If children are not permitted to swim with a parent during adult swim, just swim there when it's not too crowded. Support the new swimmer as you both walk in the water together.

After the swimmer is comfortable with walking in the water, let them walk without your assistance.

Walk with hands always underwater. Pulling the water, with hands underwater, is similar to swimming. Swimmers will learn that pulling water with their hands helps them to move in the water. This movement is similar to the hand motion of the breaststroke.

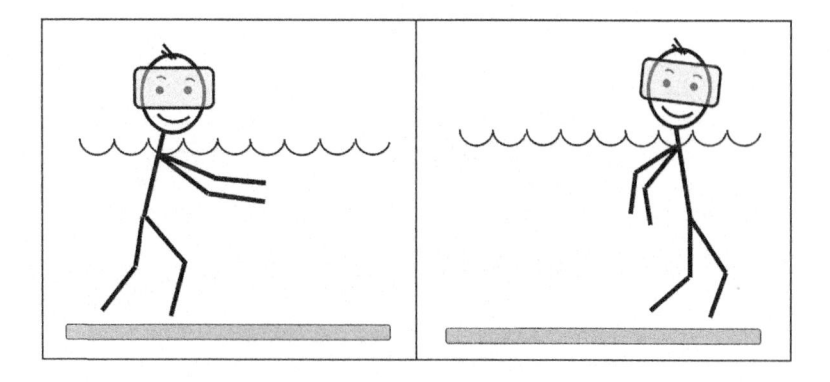

Try walking with hands underwater for pulling but use an out-of-water return. This movement is similar to the hand motion of the American Crawl.

Try racing with hands always underwater and then with hands out of the water. Which way is faster?

Before asking your child to jump to you, get into the pool first and just pick up your child from the edge of the pool.

Whirl your child around, splashing just their feet in the water. Absolutely no face splashes. Then, hold your child on your hip and let them dangle their feet in the water. Just take a walk in the shallow water.

When your child jumps to you and you whirl them around, gradually allow more splashes hit their face. Don't rush it. If your child does not like the splashes, then he/she may wear a face mask. Their first few jumps should be to you, not to the water.

Eventually, you can catch them a little later, and allow them to jump into the water. Make sure they feel safe and comfortable. When your child can jump in, without your assistance, ask him/her to walk or doggy paddle to you. If they want to keep wearing their face mask, that's fine. It should be their decision if and when they no longer want to wear it.

Warning: Jumping into the shallow end of the pool is an important skill to master, but it can be dangerous too. So, be careful. When children first try to jump into the shallow end, they get a little nervous and stiffen up. Tell your child to bend their knees as they jump so they will have a nice, soft landing. I once saw a small girl jump into the shallow end with stiff legs. She landed with her legs completely straight and hurt her knees. It certainly did not add to her joy of swimming.

Some advice on advice: When giving advice, tell your child what to do. Don't tell them what not to do. They will focus on what you tell them, so simply tell them what to do. (e.g. Don't say "Don't keep your legs straight." Tell them "Bend your knees.")

Swimming under a parent's legs is another way to get the feel of the water. Swimming through and pulling on legs is similar to swimming underwater and pulling on just the water.

While your child is wearing a face mask, ask them to swim under your legs. For the first few attempts, the parent will do all the work. Your child will put his/her head down low but the head may not be completely submerged. Just kick your leg up and over your child and rotate so your child has gone through your legs. Ask your child to try to grab your knees and pull through your legs. Eventually, they will get the idea. In time, they will be able to submerge, grab your knees and pull through your legs. After they have mastered swimming through your legs, ask your child to swim through the legs of two people.

Avoid using flotation devices. They give the child an abnormal feel of the water. The only exception is small water wings. They provide a little support and do not significantly affect the child's body position and movement in the water.

In addition to swimming under a parent's legs, there are many other things a child can do in the shallow end of the pool. Encourage and help your child to try the following:

- Pull yourself down the rungs of the ladder. Very young children are buoyant and have difficulty staying down. By holding onto the ladder, they can stay under water more easily.

- Pickup things at the bottom of the pool (e.g. coins and small toys that sink).

- Try floating on your back. At first, the parent should gently hold the child's head and support their back as needed. The parent should make sure it is a pleasant experience. Make sure no pool waves cover the child's face.

- Try swimming (doggy paddle) from the wall to the parent. Encourage your child to push off from the wall and keep their face above water (for comfort).

- If there is a shallow area where they can stand with their head above the water, ask them to use their arms and hands to run. Arms and hands must stay under water. This movement is similar to regular swimming movements.

Float on Your Back

Help the swimmer get into a floating position by providing minimal support behind the shoulders and head. Encourage the swimmer to move slowly. Quick movements will cause splashes. Make sure the swimmer's face stays above water.

Age 4
Swim Lesson

Feet on the Ground

Children may have difficulty changing from a back float to standing because awkward movements may cause uncomfortable splashes.

To change from a back floating position to a standing position may be difficult for some swimmers. The following things should be done in order, and almost simultaneously:
- Reach back, grab water, and pull your hands forward.
- Tuck your knees to your chest.
- Lift your head.
- The motion is like reaching back to grab a chair then sitting on it.

Help the swimmer with getting their feet to the ground.

Doggy Paddle

Encourage your child to swim to you. Doing a doggy paddle is fine. Praise them for "swimming" because they are swimming! As they develop skill and confidence, move farther away.

If you do not feel comfortable doing this in deep water, ask a lifeguard to take your place.

Jump In

When the swimmer is comfortable with going into a back float to a standing position, unassisted, show them how to jump into the water from the side of the pool. Start with sitting on the edge of the shallow water and scooting in. Then jump from the edge. Try running in the shallow water, using arms and hands to help. Also try doggy paddling.

When the swimmer is comfortable in the shallow end of the pool (about 3 feet deep) progress to deeper water. Eventually, the swimmer should be able to jump off the diving board and doggy paddle to the edge.

After spending time with you in the shallow water, your child will naturally become interested in going to other parts of the pool. Let them hold onto your shoulders while you swim to the deeper parts of the pool (4 or 5 feet deep).

In the shallow end, let your child practice swimming short distances to you. Don't worry about their stroke. A simple doggy paddle is fine. Repeat this activity in deeper water to build confidence.

At this point, your child may still want to wear their face mask. That's fine. It should be their decision if and when they no longer want to wear their mask. Believe me, they will get tired of it!

In the deep end of the pool, let your child jump in and swim to you. Let them hold onto your shoulders while you doggy paddle or do the breast stroke to swim around together. When your child becomes a stronger swimmer, still doing a doggy paddle, let him/her follow you as you swim around the pool. Of course, keep an eye on your child and hold them up if they start to tire.

Jumping off the board should be requested by the child. They will see all the "big kids" jumping off the board and want to do that too.

When my son asked me if he could jump off the board, I told him he would not be allowed to wear his mask. He quickly decided that he did not need the mask.

To prepare your child for jumping off the board, let your child jump from the edge of the pool, without their mask, into the deep water (e.g. 5 feet deep). Of course, you should be in the water, waiting for them, as usual. After they jump in and doggy paddle to you, give them a push and let them doggy paddle back to the edge of the pool.

If you do not feel comfortable in the deeper water with your child, hire a lifeguard to work/swim with your child.

When you both feel the child is ready to jump off the diving board, walk to the end of the board and jump off the board first. Then ask your child to walk to the end of the board and jump off. If they don't feel comfortable jumping, they may sit down and scoot off the edge of the diving board. The parent should stay in the water, about 5 feet from the edge of the board. After your child jumps in, quickly grab and pull them up. Then push your child towards the edge. They should doggy paddle to the edge and climb up the ladder. They will probably want to repeat this again and again!

Eventually, your child will want to jump off the board, without your waiting for him or her in the water. Practice a few times, with you in the water, but do not touch your child. Instead, let them jump off the board, come to the surface, and doggy paddle directly to the ladder, without your help.

When you feel your child is safe, stand at the edge of the pool, while your child jumps off the board and doggy paddles to the edge, without any assistance.

Jumping off of a diving board and doggy paddling to the edge without assistance is a major milestone for any swimmer. It indicates the child is comfortable and safe in the water. At this point, a child's comfort and confidence around the water will grow.

Age 3 Jumping

A year after my son jumped off the diving board without assistance, he wanted to swim to the bottom of the pool. My concern was that if he swam to the bottom of the 10 foot deep water and simply touched the bottom with his hand, he would not have enough strength and time to return to the top. He needed to put his feet on the bottom and push upward. We practiced together and I made sure he put his feet on the bottom so he could push upward. If he got into trouble, I was there to help push him upward. After preliminary testing with me underwater and nearby, he showed me that he could place his feet on the bottom and push upward.

When I felt comfortable, I let him jump off the diving board, go to the bottom, and push upward, all by himself.

By the time my son was 4-years-old, he had developed a very good feel of the water.

For an extra challenge and excitement, I often took my son to water parks. We swam together in wave pools and slid down big slides. I always went down the slides first and waited for him at the end.

Warning: Be careful with water slides. Tell your child to cross their legs, cross their arms across their chest and to lift their head, while sliding. This keeps their head from banging the slide during the sharp turns and during the drop at the end. Tell them to keep their head slightly lifted up.

Using flotation devices at water parks is a lot of fun. I do not like the use of flotation devices while a child is learning to swim, but after they can move in the water fairly well, I think flotation devices are great fun.

Age 7
Lazy
River

[2] Swimming in the Water

Jumping off a diving board and doggy paddling to the edge is a good, first step in learning to swim. At this point, the swimmer is ready to learn to swim with proper technique. There are many swim programs that will refine and improve your child's swimming skills.

I am qualified to teach swimming and thought I would teach my son to swim. But, I mostly just taught him to enjoy the water and to doggy paddle. He learned most of his swimming techniques, beyond doggy paddling, from other swim instructors and swim coaches.

My son never considered me a source of swimming information. I was just his swimming buddy. He wanted to swim faster and take swim lessons from a lifeguard at the local pool. He also enjoyed group swim lessons with his friends.

I recommend enrolling your child in a local swim program. If possible, enroll your child in group and private swim lessons. My son had his first private swim lesson when he was four-years-old.

Formal swim lessons should not be started until your child is already comfortable and safe in the water. If formal swim lessons are started before a child is comfortable in the water, the swimmer will find the lessons stressful. If a child is already comfortable in the water, swim lessons will significantly improve his/her swimming ability and confidence in the water.

Children who have been taught proper swimming techniques are more likely to enjoy swimming as a lifelong sport.

Age 12
Freestyle

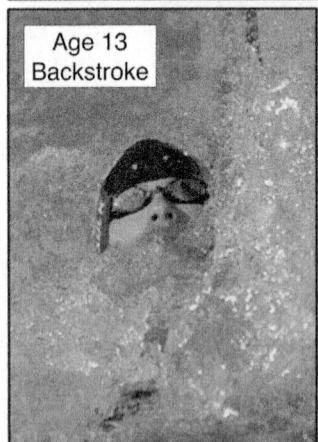

Age 13
Backstroke

Age 13
Breaststroke

Age 13
Butterfly

[3] Swimming Fast

Children who enjoy swimming will probably want to learn how to swim faster. But, your child may prefer a different sport or hobby. Don't push. Expose your child to a variety of sports and hobbies and see what sticks. Support them in any direction they take.

There are many things parents can do to support their child in sports. However, family resources will limit what parents can reasonably do.

Participating in multiple sports may be chaotic. For example, my son would wear his swim suit under his Tae Kwon Do (TKD) uniform because swim practice was immediately after TKD practice.

If your child is a swimming enthusiast, by the time they are teenagers (in middle school), swimming will take up so much of time that there will be little time to pursue any other sport. The other sports may became hobbies and swimming may became their passion.

40

BASKETBALL	SOCCER	GYMNASTICS
BASEBALL	PIANO	VIOLIN
SNOW SKIING	TAE KWON DO	TENNIS

Supporting any child in any sport requires a lot of time and money. If grandparents or other relatives are available to help, they can take the child to some practices and/or competitions. If extra family members are not available, parents often coordinate driving with other parents. It's a huge time commitment and parents with several children may find it difficult to support all of their children as fully as they would like.

My husband and I had only child, so we were able to give him a lot of support. Also, since my husband traveled a lot for his work, I was not able to work full-time. Since I was a full-time-mom and had only one child, I had the time needed to drive my son to all of his swim practices.

When your swimmer is old enough to drive a car, he can drive himself to swim practice. In some ways that's a relief, in other ways, it's a worry!

Swim Teams

Many children will enjoy the fun and excitement of swimming with their friends on a local, competitive, and/or school swim team. When a child swims on a swim team, he/she will spend more time swimming and that will naturally make them better and faster swimmers.

Age 7
Ribbons
& Trophy

Children may join a local or <u>summer swim team</u> when they are five or six. Each local swimming pool may have a team. Swim practices are usually held in the morning, before the pool opens. Lifeguards, who the children idolize, usually manage the team. Swim meets are held once or twice a week. The dual meets involve two competing, local swim teams. At the end of the summer, a championship meet, involving many local swim teams is held. Parents bring food and cookies and the focus is on having fun. There is some competition, but it is minimal. Many ribbons are given. Overall, the meets are informal and fun.

Age 10 Summer Swim Team

Age 11
Competitive
Swim Team

Competitive swim teams often practice at a high school. Competitive swim teams are associated with an area of the country. Like their name suggests, they are competitive. All swimmers are ranked and timed. To find a competitive swim team, look online at USAswimming.org or Swimming.org.

Swim practices for young swimmers are usually held after school. Older swimmers practice for several hours, twice a day for a total of about 4 hours per day, six days a week.

It's fun to chat with the other parents at swim practice while your child burns up all their energy! Swim practices are interesting to watch, for the first few years. The swim drills are organized and coordinated by the swim coaches. Each swim lane is divided into two, narrow, one-way lanes.

Participating on a competitive swim team may be very time consuming and very rewarding. Trained coaches help to improve a young swimmer's swim strokes. Swim clinics may be held, at an extra cost, to focus on swim technique. Swim practices develop both technique and endurance.

Age 14
Competitive
Swim Team

Children are usually very proud to swim competitively. They will enjoy going to swim meets and hanging out with friends. Competitive swim meets usually last four or five hours. When meets are held at public schools, families often camp out on blankets, in the school gym. When meets are held at outdoor pools during the summer, families sit on benches and blankets around the pool. The children play games, while waiting for their events. The competitive meets are very official and exciting. Official swim times are recorded online and the swimmers are ranked nationally.

Most competitive swim meets are held locally. Some larger competitive swim meets are farther away and teams travel on a bus. These meets are more selective, and qualifying times may be required to participate. At these larger swim meets, the parents and visitors usually sit in the bleachers while the swimmers stay on the pool deck with their coaches and swim team.

Age 16
Breaststroke

Qualifying swimmers, may compete in national swim meets. National and Junior National meets are held at the end of the summer swim season.

Age 17 Junior Nationals

In the United States, High school swim teams are like any high school sports team. They help children have fun while they learn hard work pays off. They also learn sportsmanship and other life skills. The extra swimming and coaching will improve their swimming.

Age 17
High School
Swim Team

While in high school, many swimmers train and compete with their competitive swim team for most of the year (May through December). Then they train and compete with their high school swim team, during the high school swim season (January through April). Most of the high school meets are dual meets, held during a weekday evening, between two local high schools.

In the United States, the high school swim season culminates with regional and statewide competition, however, swimmers must qualify to participate in these meets.

At a High School States Championship meet, the maximum number of events per swimmer is four. I am proud to say that my son won four gold medals at states.

Age 18

HS State Championship Meet

After high school, my son swam on a Division 1 college swim team.

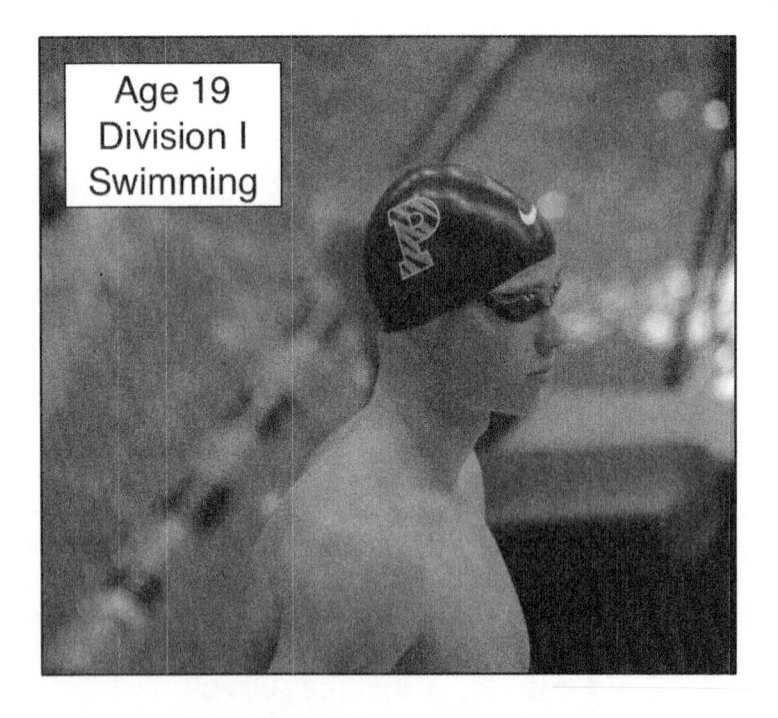

After college, swimmers may compete on a masters swim team. For more information, search online for Masters Swimming. (usms.org or swimming.org/masters/).

Advanced Swim Lessons

While swimming on a competitive swim team, my son had a private swim lesson, from the coach, once a week. Paying for private lessons, in addition to team fees, swim meet fees, swim camp fees, equipment fees, and travel fees adds up quickly. Swimming, like any sport, can be very time consuming and expensive. However, they will significantly improve a swimmer's technique.

Colleges often sponsor swim camps for young swimmers. Check local universities for swim camps near you.

Private swim lessons are often available from the team coach or assistant coach. Private lessons may also be provided by good swimmers, from local schools and universities. Just ask!

One parent asked a lifeguard, where my son swims, for a swim-tutor recommendation. The lifeguard recommended my son because he had seen him swim and knew about his swimming experience. The parent contacted my son to arrange a private swim lesson for his child. My son enjoyed working with the young swimmer who, I'm sure, got some very good tips.

Additional Support

Being on a competitive swim team takes a lot of time. During middle and high school, swimmers will practice about 2 hours before school and 2 hours after school. They often spend over four hours at swim practice, every day. It's difficult to keep up with school work with a time commitment like that.

My son ate half of his breakfast, in the car, on the way to before-school (morning) swim practice. Then, after practice, he ate the other half, in the car, while I drove him to school.

The after-school (evening) swim practice starts about an hour after kids get home from school. If you can drive your child home after school, you can eliminate bus time. With the extra time, your child will have time to do their homework, before evening swim practice. To provide extra support, consider using tutors to help your child with their homework. If possible, tutor them yourself.

I always picked up my son, after school and drove him directly to swim practice. We sat in the car, ate a healthy snack, and did his homework together for about 1.5 hours, before swim practice started. Since I have strong math background, we spent most of the time, working on math homework.

When my son decided swimming was more important than doing his homework, he would jump out of the car and run to swim practice without completing his homework. My solution to this was to simply park the car several miles away from swim practice so that he could not escape. He knew that I would not take him to swim practice until all of his math homework was completed.

By the time he got to high school, our homework-before-evening-swim-practice system had become a habit. During the high school swim season, my son had swim practice at his high school. During the 2 hours after school and before swim practice, I drove to his high school and we did his homework, together, in the car. As usual, we focused on his math homework because I have a strong math background. If I was not able to help him, I would have used math tutors to help him. Math tutors can help any child do better in math, regardless of the students' ability and level.

In my mind, it was academics first and swimming second. In my son's mind, it was swimming first and academics second. Our system of doing homework, in the car, before evening swim practice allowed us to avoid conflict. If you are not comfortable helping your swimmer with their schoolwork, you can schedule tutor sessions after school and before the evening swim practice.

Your child will appreciate being able to keep up with their academics but may become frustrated with your insistence of completing all homework before going to his evening swim practice. Doing well academically and having good swim times will make your child an attractive candidate at many universities.

Finally, these days, my son thanks me for making him do and helping him with his math homework before evening swim practices. It was the support he needed to prepare him for rigorous academics at the university level while swimming on a Division 1 swim team.

ACKNOWLEDGEMENTS

I'd like to thank my son for all of his hard work and dedication to the sport of swimming. My husband and I provided a lot of support but he did all the work. It was a joy to be part of his swimming journey and we'd do it all over again, if given the chance.

I'd like to thank my husband for his behind-the-scenes support. He was at work while I drove our son to swim practice and he attended all the swim meets with me.

Mostly, I'd like to thank my own parents for teaching me how to swim. With seven children, my parents had their hands full. My mother did not know how to swim and was a little fearful of the water. My father was a good swimmer and instinctively knew to simply put his children in the water, keep them safe, and let them learn to enjoy the water. My parents never pushed. They simply put us in small backyard pools and in the shallow section of public pools. All of my brothers and sisters and I know how to swim. We grew up enjoying the water and have passed the joy of swimming to our own children.

Printed in Great Britain
by Amazon